Copyright © 2019 High Priestesses of Poetry. All rights reserved.
Poems copyright their respective authors.

Grateful acknowledgment to the editors of the following publications in which some of these poems first appeared, sometimes in different versions:
Levure Littéraire: "Addendum To Blood Moon Eclipse Over the Pacific"
The Journal of Feminist Studies in Religion: "Fire"
Journal of Feminist Studies: "Meditations on The I Ching, Hexagrams 2 & 43"
TQ14: "Menopause"

HIGH PRIESTESSES
of POETRY

an anthology

2018

VOLUME ONE

ASH GOOD

BETH MELNICK

DAWN THOMPSON

GABRIELLE HANCHER

HOLADAY MASON

JENN LALIME

K.M. LIGHTHOUSE

LAUREN PAREDES

RHONDA NICHOLS

♦

"When women circle, something magical happens . . .
What makes a circle special?
Being known beyond the roles that define us,
speaking our dreams into existence,
mourning what's been lost,
a container for promises,
recognition that we are valued,
time for honoring our innate connection
to the cycles of the earth,
the moment of recognition when we hear
our own truth spoken by another,
a space to call our own."

— KRISTEN RODERICK

introduction

WE FIND OURSELVES in the midst of an upside-down and misdirected epoch, so even more dire is the call to rise as our own healers, consecrate our existence by making art in community and grow our own utopias. High Priestesses of Poetry came to me in a vision—a journey of word channeled and spoken in fellowship that would offer a renewed wholeness to those who circled to play.

In my utopia we are the story tellers who gather to ring our voices in truth and love to heal one another. We own our privileges and protect the knowledge of our collective pasts. We pre-tend the future with sustainable practices that respect all human lineages and the timeless wisdom of plant, animal, mineral and space bodies. We are present—the time markers of breathing seasons. We know ourselves as speakers of magic who conjure laughter, tears and remembrance. When we offer our witness to intuitive intelligence, we are High Priestesses.

When I shared this vision with my writing community, astounding women heeded the call. We gathered in online ritual as a coven without walls on the Spring Equinox, Summer Solstice, Fall Equinox and Winter Solstice in 2018.

These seasonal circles became a potent threshold for spiritual osmosis. What we experienced in the outer world was pulled in as source material, digested and witnessed. What we created in our inner sanctuary nourished our emerging relationships, inspired our craft and reflected meaning back out into our lives.

The pages of this anthology will be unable to fully capture the spectrum of alchemy that we experienced, but the stories offered here are powerful testaments in their own right. I chose to order our poems by the moods of the Moon, our great sky reminder that there is a right time and place for all things. You may notice how our voices breath into one another in the tides of inspiration that push and pull through this body of writing, offering affirmation that in the faceted surfaces of others' stories, we can find a mirror to our own stories.

May this sharing of our play, of our circle's story, in some way point you toward the power and possibility of staking claim to your own utopias, of finding your people.

To my dearest High Priestesses: my deepest gratitude to each of you for arriving in the right time and place to so generously offer the unearthed diamonds of your stories and claim your place in the co-creation of this magic. I am awed to know your poetic voices in this dimension. May you continually share your light and intuition where it is respected and honored in this world. ♦

ASH GOOD
INITIATRIX, HIGH PRIESTESSES OF POETRY

EMPTY / *new moon*

23   Doppelgänger
Lauren Paredes

24   What Priestesses Gathered in the Web Say About Spring
Holaday Mason

26   The Mother Keeps Calling Her Baby
Ash Good

28   On the Business of Being Born
Gabrielle Hancher

30   Nothing to Say
Beth Melnick

31   When She Started She Didn't Want Someone Dying Just to Get Her Wish
Ash Good

34   We Can Imagine That It Must Have Trembled Before It Fell
Lauren Paredes

37   Empty is a Good Place to Start
Beth Melnick

INTENTION / *waxing crescent moon*

41   Birthing
Dawn Thompson

43   What She Really Wants to Talk About is Undoing
Ash Good

46	Meditations on the I Ching, Hexagrams 2 & 43 *Holaday Mason*	
49	We Float in the Air Though We Are Worlds Made of Stone *K. M. Lighthouse*	
51	I Never Stopped Writing You Love Letters, Dear One *Ash Good*	
53	In the Company of Priestess Women, I Remember I Am One *K. M. Lighthouse*	

MOVEMENT / *first quarter moon*

57	A Memory *Gabrielle Hancher*	
59	I Do Not Yet Know *Lauren Paredes*	
60	Going *Rhonda Nichols*	
62	Agency *Jenn Lalime*	
63	And yet . . . *Beth Melnick*	
65	Fire *Holaday Mason*	
67	She Asks Me Not to Call Her Judy *K. M. Lighthouse*	

69	Permission *Gabrielle Hancher*
71	Medial *Lauren Paredes*
72	Three Years Into This Pain I Carry *K. M. Lighthouse*
74	Rest in Motion *Beth Melnick*

REFINEMENT / *waxing gibbous moon*

81	Gut Feelings are Guardian Angels *Lauren Paredes*
83	Someone We Once Knew We Now Know *Holaday Mason*
85	Expanded by Sri Yantra *K. M. Lighthouse*
86	How Does a Mother Find Time to Write a Poem? *Dawn Thompson*
88	"We Must Lower Our Standard of Living So We Can Raise Our Standard of Loving" *K. M. Lighthouse*
91	One Day My Kitchen Will Be Clean *Jenn Lalime*
93	"This Is How She Prays; Clean Is Whom She Prays To" *K. M. Lighthouse*
95	Coming Home *Gabrielle Hancher*

RELEASE / *full moon*

101	Urban Prayer	*Gabrielle Hancher*
103	Seasons	*Dawn Thompson*
107	What Now?	*Jenn Lalime*
113	Addendum to Blood Moon Eclipse Over The Pacific	*Holaday Mason*
115	Stars Fall Down	*Beth Melnick*
118	Solstice	*Gabrielle Hancher*
119	For Hye	*Jenn Lalime*
121	The Dying are Good Children to the Dead	*Holaday Mason*

GRATITUDE / *waning gibbous moon*

127	A New Look	*Gabrielle Hancher*
128	When Women Circle	*Ash Good*
129	Winter Circle	*Rhonda Nichols*

130	The Crone Gives a Pedicure	
	Dawn Thompson	
132	I Don't Know You	
	Ash Good	
133	Ancient Mother	
	Rhonda Nichols	
135	Suddenly Every Sound is a Love Song	
	Lauren Paredes	

FORGIVENESS / *last quarter moon*

139	Her Cosmos of Hearths, This Settling	
	Ash Good	
142	Winter Solstice: The Last View	
	Holaday Mason	
146	On the Subject of Self Care	
	Gabrielle Hancher	
148	What Follows	
	Jenn Lalime	
150	Mercury Moves Like a Stone Rolled in Front of the Cave	
	Ash Good	
152	Worthy	
	Rhonda Nichols	
154	"My Mother's Voice, That Imperfect Love"	
	Ash Good	

SURRENDER / *waning crescent moon*

159   Annie
Rhonda Nichols

161   The Beloved
Dawn Thompson

164   The Circle
Beth Melnick

166   Something Heroic About Curling Into a Fetal Position to Hold the Multiverse Under the Bed
Ash Good

168   Right in Front of You
Jenn Lalime

170   Be Soft a Little Longer
Lauren Paredes

172   In These Nested Eggs, May We Never Harden
K. M. Lighthouse

174   Menopause
Holaday Mason

175   They Stepped Back Into the Arms of the Infinite
Beth Melnick

BEGINNING / *new moon*

179   Rebirth
Rhonda Nichols

181	"It's All a Gift, You Decide"
Lauren Paredes
182	Until the Notion of Other Cannot be Parsed Separate at All
Ash Good
185	The Alchemist
Gabrielle Hancher
186	When She
Holaday Mason
191	**BIOGRAPHIES**

empty

new moon

LAUREN PAREDES

Doppelgänger

I step into the electric field hoping
it initiates some awakening,

that when tulips & goldenrod are done
with me I'll be so infused with vitality

that some passerby will do a doubletake,
& mistake me for springtime.

◆

What Priestesses Gathered in the Web Say About Spring

Mostly the women talk of the reprieve from rain,
of sunlight & gauzy peach blooms, starting tulips,
diaphanous ranunculus pushing—a strong hunger to kneel
in the mud, wet kneed in blue jeans, sun
on their winter shoulders, troweling the dirt,
turning dark things up, startled as they should be
to suddenly see the light.
     As a toddler I often sat in the pathway
to my mother's door, staring at the faces of pansies,
which seemed gnomes, bearded men with eyes crossed,
brows scowling. I wouldn't let them know they scared me
& they never told their secrets, which by nature closed
every evening as the shadow of the house carved
itself across the lawn behind me, day released
as if a great lung were exhaling.

                    Unassumingly, the women say
they still need soft shawls to ward off the remaining chill
as they dig in the earth, planting & tending, but they don't
reveal the hues of their wraps or the names
of the still leafless trees they love. For now, they murmur
mainly of relief, rejoicing in the absence of bone chill,
celebrating the sticky umber soil between their fingers—
earth calming that enduring human fear that winter might
go on forever, reveling in the way warmth liberates
peace, peace as reassuring as a man humming easy at his work
nearby, the memory of summer waking in the piqued smell
of spring mud, warmth easing the aches of arms, of thighs.
From afar, I watch how pale green halos gather around
each woman's face in the coming on of the light, the continuing.

◆

ASH GOOD

The Mother Keeps Calling Her Baby

> *"You once lay there, the vernix not yet wiped off,*
> *and someone gazed at you as if you were the first*
> *sunrise seen from the Earth"*
> —Ellen Bass, "Gate C22"

too soon she is too old to be held
around the same time she insists

she can add up her own dice & it's hard
to retract stakes of independence

before this she is easy to love
freshly melted toward

the mother's warm skin
doesn't brace for lips to lips

she can't give the mother advice
because it will be fourteen more moons

until she mouths whole sentences
after her arrival first makes arms mother

what her weight feels like
how she squirms but also settles breath-still

the mother wrung-done from the potion
of turning inside out under fluorescent

which nurse is kindest & how the crone
likely takes over regardless

the mother's face is blurry
she cannot see how the mother must look at her

tiny in some perfectly average way
wrinkled, blue-irised & somehow every bit of her

but almost none of her yet
the mother is watching

intimate with the carefully-tucked
anarchy in her small-boned body

♦

GABRIELLE HANCHER

On the Business of Being Born

I'm in darkness
It's my first time in this place
Or else I've been here before
I think maybe I'm being born
But when I ask the universe puts a finger to my lips
And starts braiding chlorophyll into my hair

I would say it's a lot like the Womb
But I've never been there
Or else I have but the memory leaves a blank hole
Where my mind will someday form
And I'm left wondering
If they really did stop dinner for my arrival

It's possible I'm screaming
But the sound is muffled by dirt
Or else I have no mouth
And the business of being born is a strange one
When you can't quite remember the notes
But they keep asking you to sing

Despite all of this organized cosmic chaos
My roots grow down
Or else those are my legs
And the universe begins to hum
My real name over and over and over again
Until I'm certain that there's nothing left to do but grow upwards
Towards what I will soon remember is the Sun

Blooming isn't easy,
And a lot of people
Have done it
Before you

♦

BETH MELNICK

Nothing to Say

There is nothing to say, that comes from me.
Rome is burning and I wait for a sign.
I hold my hands open.
Along with my heart I notice beauty.
I hold my child and kiss my husband, more.
You never know when things will change and . . .

There is nothing to say that comes from me.
I read what better men and women have said or written
I hope some of them infuse some of me.
I pray that god holds hands and I reach out.
A preemptive bid.

There is nothing to say that comes from me.
The harsh rise, blotting out the subtle.
Yet the most beautiful people I have known
had so little and shared so much.
I want to be better and I think
maybe
there is still time.

♦

ASH GOOD

When She Started She Didn't Want Someone Dying Just to Get Her Wish

outside a halo of ritual she cuts a watermelon
small enough to hold in her palm

blushing flesh speckled
with unexpected anomalies that strike at the oddness

of prizing seedless for convenience
life swirls across her tongue roughness

& she avoids cracking potential
by spitting the memory of motherhood out

one long bubbly stretch of saliva
since she cannot stomach this intelligence

humility rises pink, featherless
& yawning for feeding

within the wild wingspan of anima at its strongest
fixed to a ceaseless pyre of reform & dissolution

she is the taut & bunched center loosening at edges
so the gerbera is not dead but dying & she

is here longer only she is younger than this flower
essence at the threshold of formless

the stem is severed but still sips from the vessel
left at the door with a note by the wise man

who is also tracking death
& they both can feel it

she caresses the head which calls to her & is
smooth & wrinkled & living & dying & young & old &

everything that she also is
& so she admits a guiltless tryst with this blossom

to her lover who she promises no fidelity
to the cosmos which would never expect it

she returns to forgotten roots & dips her fingers in
an earthworm passage to witness history

of what she has nurtured to be stunning
but not always nutritious & this mortal must eat

she helps earth swallow a fistful of pliable sources
waters & wishes for transformation

when a fledgling seeks daylight
she is at once in a puddle of the mother's

satin & old clairvoyant fingers
folding the mother's gown to tuck in her own closet

she knows she is worthy
when she is both

weathered trunk
& pliable green body

♦

LAUREN PAREDES

We Can Imagine That It Must Have Trembled Before It Fell

i. Goddess Kali has been after me for a whole
year now. What will I give her for our anniversary,
and what will she gift me? It's likely we'll see
mutual fire and a belated *I told you so—*
she's known of my tendency to destroy softly,
and hatch over and over.

ii. Today I found my wishbone. Am I a real woman yet?
     One who holds men accountable
     for their reckless breadcrumbing,
     their ego-riddled bodies starving for soulness
     at my watery expense?

iii. These white wings vibrate toward a different sort of surrender—
to inspire the transformation to weightlessness,
and the courage to try in the first place.

♦

BETH MELNICK

Empty is a Good Place to Start

Stay
Watch
Listen

Reflections on the ceiling
Water light
Empty, slow circles around
Myself, or where I thought I was

Empty hands
Open
Lungs open
Loose and ...

It would be sad
It feels sad
Except

Empty is a good place to start

intention

waxing crescent moon

DAWN THOMPSON

Birthing

I watch the tulips stretch their necks
toward the cold March light,
an ancestral memory somewhere deep in their roots
of crossing over to blossom.

Just last week the daffodils
showed up for the party in silk dresses
an hour early outside our front door,
only to be brought to their knees the next morning
by a late snow.

Sometimes it is like this.
We try and try for hope.
We want to believe when spring comes
the new life we are sure is waiting inside
will finally break us open,
out of the old seed we planted long ago.

Once upon a time we were flowering maiden legs
which took us anywhere.

Now we are these mature hips, wide like oak trees,
pushing, pushing
the greater Self out once again.

Can you hear her screams?

Can you feel how
the red rose
waiting inside last season's skin
wants her garden?

◆

What She Really Wants to Talk About is Undoing

her small ears hear the crone recite local things
with exotic names—azalea & rhododendron

her favorite flower is a daisy then
some chase for elegance turns star gazer

white long stem callas—pert shoots
twenty-four in a spray a boy buys

affection counted in chocolate covered strawberries
until you bring the whole forest in a single

pine cone that fills an entire backpack
potential sapling wins over $300 vase of soon-dead lilies

her favorite flower changes
so does her taste in humans

now gladiolas even not on sale
chamomile bunches not bought by someone else

eucalyptus leaves drying in the shower
her room a mess & still unpacking

bed pulled away from wall heater
a homeless chair that doesn't fit

well-meaning plans to recover it
backyard flamingo blown over by wind

she never leaves the muumuu
rain comes & light goes again

drinks wine & watches a need
for permeability—

to touch some place pristine & unreported
where unnamed territory of

self is a regenerating mirage
& a break in cataloging might be appropriate

she reclaims the walkway home
with deer skin protection

unroots nettles
asks of the spiral to let go of the soil

looseness in her holding
thank you after

she lets the man at the dispensary suggest
flower he thinks will please

says nothing of his offer
asks for what she knows she will want

♦

Meditations on the I Ching, Hexagrams 2 & 43

for LW

It was always as if someone were watching—

like a mare, in placid field.
Yet, it was always . . . just me.

Fog smears the nearly full moon.

I reach up through
three black limbs

& three petals
undone by my touch,
drift to earth—

but first caress my face.

Was I so careless, demons always

at the edges, impossible

to still—like weeds?

Such an effort to keep things
manicured—

The frog pond is an opera—
the murky dank of eucalyptus, huge.

You can't make someone
speak who does not want to.

& silence has its bells—

one each minute, hour, in octaves

you must discern.

Everything will eventually arrive.

Eventually, a squeaky bike at dawn,

the rider bent & focused as a snake.

Eventually, one hot blood rose
knocking on the door of sky.

In due time, a small girl
washing her hands at a coiled garden hose
—the water, oblivious, calm.

Bells. Bells.

What to do with these restless hands?

My windows open to islands far off.

I am watching *you*, you red morning birds,
am standing here just as naked.

In this simple light,
that sole blooming tree snows
as softly as a good night's sleep.

It is a prayer.

♦

K.M. LIGHTHOUSE

We Float in the Air Though We Are Worlds Made of Stone

This is something like a dream
when a sacred sister tugs with one finger

against the inside of pelvic bone
and induces a vision of a burgundy geode

I see later in altar to Ganesh,
who whispers, *look at me*

from underwater. So I open my eyes
even though I am a child again, afraid even

of water up nose, but somehow,
these contact lenses do not disappear

into their watery surroundings
when I see this rock

from the blurry vision before, blurry again
underwater but more clear

in my memory later because I listen,
listen three times with varying depths

of breath, sink to the bottom
in warm wellspring water, and wonder

how this breath appeases an elephant god.
When I learn the name of my vision stone,

I pair citrine fragments
and exchange one for art before two more sets

become gifts to other lovers,
the six of us connected

to future memory as we emerge
from the waters of mind,

becoming people-fires to light these stones
with sun as it revolves

around time.

♦

I Never Stopped Writing You Love Letters, Dear One

but for some reason, months ago, I stopped sending them. Maybe because that small me under covers in a too-small bedroom on the other side of the stairs got scared again. That small me who overheard giggling and miscalculated that to enter a room would disrupt the play. That small me who stays safe alone.

I am unsure why there is this love here and I have trouble showing it. So here—here are the letters that flowed in the afterglow of each time we opened a portal. Here are the ways I see you under your costumes and admire your beauty, how others agree when I say you are special—here from far away, so sure of your mission. How the light even comes through your skin different.

A being visited me in a dream last week—a woman sure in her body and soft, a foreigner, like me, in transit on a magic bus making terminal rounds through an intergalactic airport. She curled up to me on the bench seat and I was free to love her, to be loved. And upon waking it was impossible to tell if this being was myself. If this being was you. If the permission to love myself and the permission to love you could ever be separate.

You is so expansive and becomes everyone. How this story is so old, I begin to see I can write it to so many women. How I just want to curl up with me, curl up with *you* when the softness visits. The tragedy of any love letter left unsent.

Again and again your stories swallow and flash freeze a non-lasting ripple of my being so that I might see. That you might tenderly hold the gift of how much I am nourished by your senses. How much I love being in your stories. How your stories are my favorite love letters.

◆

K.M. LIGHTHOUSE

In the Company of Priestess Women, I Remember I Am One

When we gather on the equinox,
a woman holds a bottle up to camera light
and creates rainbows in these retina displays
of sacred web conference where we are only hologram,
experiment endowed with consciousness projected into morning,
filtered though lenses and layers over crystal
to form some imagined solid
and now, too, the elusive dawn that is aurora in every language—
delicate to earth but strong to cosmos. We are all
those in our projection, mobiles of crystal kaleidoscope transmissions
that ache to touch ground in our wandering for new angles
of the star storm that created us,
and in the stillness of our digital breath, we are called to begin
with bells and woven blankets draped in welcome.

♦

movement

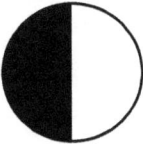

first quarter moon

GABRIELLE HANCHER

A Memory

I'm catching frogs in a fishbowl
There's at least eighty in there
Waiting for the Giant's release
And I do,
An armageddon of amphibians on the lawn

Then I'm in the river
Sliding across rocks and moss
To cure the stinging nettles
Praying a fish will touch me
Or maybe the spirit of this forest

And I'm collecting treasures
To turn into slap dash works of art
That I will finish with googly eyes in the attic
Of that tiny cottage
I'm creating small worlds
Making meaning

I'm older now and I have to go out farther
To find the magic that
At first I thought was Jesus
But as we ran,
Lungs dizzy with fresh mountain air
I realized it was just nudity

So I'm leaving these little stacks of rocks behind
Hoping maybe another dreamer might get lost out here
Making wishes on fishes
And looking for Jesus in a bowl of frogs
They'll see the way nature is so unabashed
That they'll leave behind the treasures of their heart too,
Naked and full of magic

♦

LAUREN PAREDES

I Do Not Yet Know

Which voice to listen to—
the one that says "we must hold on;
there is no other way" or the other that sings
of persistence's fruitlessness,
inviting me to outgrow
                        the nightly vigil.

Regardless,
I do not regret the alters, the rose-
water, the ghost
I fostered and then swallowed whole,
who may or may not be speaking right now.

♦

Going

I surrender to her pillows
Sleepless, exhausted
Going, going
Like stones down a mountain

Miles on a roadway
Its bumps keeping time
Like a metronome
And I am thirteen again
With bow in hand
Legs full of cello
Counting, counting time

Sister and mother
From another age
Share words and laughter
While my heart beats
In retreat to silence

Every region has its treasure
Every city its veneer
We are travelers here
Passing, passing through

♦

JENN LALIME

Agency

I'm thinking about the genesis of hate
        protection and fear and violence

        the staggering specificity of desire
        how quick we come to judgment
        how ready with pitchforks

I'm thinking about habits of exodus
        distraction and medication and escape

        the bright glow of modernity
        how we consume and follow
        how each click corrupts

I'm thinking about simpler chapters
        pavement and chalk and smooth stones

        the one legged hop, up and back again
        how we marked just one square—
        the thrill of skipping right on over it

♦

BETH MELNICK

And Yet . . .

Even as the rough connections are remade here
I see you
I imagine you
lying there, in a room so crowded with your hastily moved things

Even as the life I have built here wraps itself
a little closer around me
and its rhythm resumes
I think of you

I feel you near
So near a spark leaps from your slow burn
toward the tinder I have become

I slam the portal door
The latch doesn't catch
That spark alights inside
exploding into a full raging fire

You would burn me to the ground
I know this
and yet

I stand close to you when I can

♦

HOLADAY MASON

Fire

You never expected her to burst naked, flying from the tree
           & not a neon billboard in sight to direct you
so you must stay the course of nocturnal beauty.
~
The back of a running doe is a wave
           threading through high grass—exactly the way the woman's
spine is, as each minute is & you want the whole
~
pale length of her, from crown to cave—her skin sheet
           a sail beneath which all else is shadow—
shadow bodies everywhere, waiting to meet—but *you* knew that.
~
And, much the way the doe remains forever standing in the road—
           such is the woman's slow motion leap
as if from a fire, those dried leaves, amber confetti,
~
dripping into the dark around her body
           while the unmade bed of her red
hair swells, then nearly sweeps the broken yellow lines
~

of the highway where *you* stand so far below. She reaches
        farther & harder than you could ever
bear, her might in the tips of fingers saturated

~

with what, *you* don't know, but your *body* does
        because it feels her body flinging out between
the ground & the sky, a pale weaver suspended

~

& not a single hint of starlight—
no, she alone cuts her own white country open.

♦

K. M. LIGHTHOUSE

She Asks Me Not to Call Her Judy

A woman says the Dagara tribe believes mothers dream children
into existence and create name songs while star-gazing

so light becomes sound that becomes flesh and every baby knows
they are welcome. I don't mention the story is a hoax

because she says no song waited for her—she had been unwanted,
so she goes for surgery afraid

of anesthetic—*I don't want to be born
in an unwelcoming world again.* When she wakes

to the weighted blanket womb of gravity, friends and lovers sing
a name song to greet her, and the second world fills

with rainbow afterimages of medical cocktails—
borders for her re-entrance.

My fetal self heard AC/DC in the womb,
and Mom tells me—*forget Mozart—that's where you get your intelligence,*

and at birth, she named and nicknamed me—
a Young and Restless character and a priestess. Later, an Abba song.

When I wake from surgery that renders me infertile,
I remember nurses' names,

though they tell me I won't, and see two saviors hold hands
in welcome, but I wasn't born then.

My second birth was after guided meditation
in a yoga-studio-turned-sanctuary with the rush of freight train

and electronic wind chimes.
But now, I am reborn in each shrine made,

in every table prepared for lovers, in all these returns
from nothing's quiet consciousness.

Before birth, I am light but return as sound
saying,

you have permission to enjoy being a body, which is as good
a name song as any.

♦

GABRIELLE HANCHER

Permission

You have permission to enjoy being a body which is to say your body is the way of things here. The way goose pimples prick your spine when you listen to ASMR or the trickling downward that happens when you hear the scratch of pen on paper.

You have permission to enjoy the crunch of grapes, the juice dribbling down your chin, or the taste of fresh spring water, or the way people look at you when you're alive and bright.

You have permission to exist in the in between spaces too like the moment before you take your sock off all the way or the second before scissors close down on a new hair cut and all these things are what bring your spirit to your body.

You have permission to remember who you were or who you are and to be excited about who you are becoming and how many times you'll get to say *thank you* in this lifetime to any number of people.

You have permission to imagine kissing the sagittal line of your skull and wonder about all the odds that got you here and why nobody told you orgasms could be so amazing sooner.

You have permission to be safe. To explore the world knowing home is always there and that a lineage of great mothers watches over you chatting away and knitting dreams into sweaters or creating beautiful trouble for you to imagine.

You have permission to kiss and tell but also to keep your own secrets and to dance naked in sacred spaces but also balance a check book or say no to things that would drain you of your worth.

You have permission to be born again and again and to know that your spirit made a home in your body for some reason and the interior decorator is fabulous (even if the colors don't always seem to go together at first).

You have permission to be held here and to be loved wholly and to be honored for the wildfire you are—nothing short of the miracle of being alive.

♦

LAUREN PAREDES

Medial

If you're always in transit, returning with bits
of bread or a message on the backside of a napkin,
you're really neither here nor there, unadvancing
toward permanence, a route back through alleyways
of time, feet perched on flaking fire escapes
to voyeurize the windows of the living, two
seniors waltzing, a casual spiritual awakening,
a TV sitcom left on for comfort, *Honey I am
home, though I don't remember having ever left.*

♦

K. M. LIGHTHOUSE

Three Years Into This Pain I Carry

I ask the waking-dream mermaid
for advice, and she tells me saltwater

heals at the salinity of ocean, so I sit
in lavender and oregano salt baths

and lean in as water washes over
this body. I light two Grotto flames,

which dip lower in their votive containers,
and wonder how many days

I will take this bath at double dilution
until I need new sacrificial candles

to soothe this body. One hand over chest
and one over pubic mound, I sink

into this feeling, and pain inside this curiosity
becomes tendrils of light free

to flood the room dedicated to this purpose.
This cosmic charge,

sacred sliver of the world wound I carry,
reminds me what wellness means

in this body.
With hands in prayer position, I release

the drain that returns me to gravity—grateful
for this water wealth's relief—

and offer my own water to circulation
before the tub dries. When the full weight

of body returns, I stand, bend, thank
these candle sentinels, and pat this flesh

dry, opening a wider channel for pain
to drip through in its inevitable return.

♦

Rest in Motion

Angels' voices rise
Bubbles pop, mud splatters
Angels or fireflies, it's a question of perception

With my eyes closed I can feel
Bones inside my head shifting
I attempt to take apart the clockworks
Assembled over so many years

Picking through bones and flesh
Emotions spin out
Moths from my cereal box
So many found homes in inattention
Surprisingly easy to kill, yet once having taken hold . . .

I want to lay the pieces of my self out for examination
There, on some clean imaginary table
I find it does not really work that way
I cannot stop everything
I can only dismantle bits and observe while still in motion

I have to keep the circuit closed
The divine impulse continues to . . . pulse
Sitting, standing, lying
It feels like madness, this constant disassembling
Reworking in motion, the seating of new impulses
New parts

It looks like nothing, from the outside
I am used to changing my costumes in public
But not the gears

Inside,
Things like apples stuck with tape want to fall
Traces of ancient nodes, particles of glass protrude
Angles right and angles sharp
Sparks fly from the effort to free themselves
Parts are broken

Seeds fall in slow motion
They wave at glass particles now free as well
Love has nothing to do with this sort of falling
This enveloping rain of the pieces
Or does it

Held so long in the grasp of mind
My limber sapling arms and legs ordered
Mind shifting its plates
Hands rigid from holding so hard for so long
Feel they will break

Love, a rush of air, of cool water
Speaks
It tells you . . .

Rest there, rest in motion
Swim in the gentler pool of your tears
Look deeply, see the reflection
See past it to the soul of the pool—also a reflection

Take a breath, breathe long deep moments
Breathe in the flutter of wings at the window
There are voices, too
Look deep into the pool of your own making
Rest there, rest in motion

Return again and again to this well
Draw your hand across the surface of the blue-green

Feel the sun, the moss
This is a world of roundness and holding softly
More is just more

Be easy, rest and roll slowly
Into that pool of your own making
Rest there, rest in motion . . .

Love has everything to do with it

♦

refinement

waxing gibbous moon

LAUREN PAREDES

Gut Feelings are Guardian Angels

I don't want to be the one who finds there are no seeds
left in the rusted tin box when it's sowing season;
uncovering instead webs with spun IOUs
in the center of their silky chaos.

Did you know some people in this world,
when polled, said they've never felt wind on their scalp?
The lightness of flight after years of praying
for buoyancy.

This reminds me of the conundrum of holy matrimony
between a bird and a fish (where they might live, etc.)
And when does curiosity mistakenly oxidize
into complacency? Aunties casually martyring themselves

like candies tossed from a firetruck in the harvest parade.
All of these worries are the heavy coats I didn't intend to wear,
long after the cold had left my bones. It occurred to me
in the pilgrimage for groundedness, one could crouch

outside their home before dawn, disturb the marigolds,
massage soil into their feet, palms, asking "who are you exactly?"
until the sun, cresting dutifully at their back, responds,
"there's no need to ask; you already know."

♦

HOLADAY MASON

Someone We Once Knew We Now Know

A woman is going to come in
through the door.
A woman is going to grab
the doorknob.
The teeth of the zipper
missing teeth leave her
like a song with lost notes.
Going into the door backwards
may have done more good than harm.
Still she find the orange peels
on the table retain some perfume
regardless of the cigarette butts,
as if she had just tied the goat with
red ribbons & it had calmed down.
Exasperating yes, her confused
bi-focal, tri-focus, what she was
or perhaps is, has become, is becoming—
it is rising like a steam or a kite
or the lead foot of a defunct God.
Pair bonding is also harrowing—
the romance of noir not enough,

never more than shadows.
A woman opens the gate
as her Corazon Negro grows
a bed of blue roses.
She needs someone to cradle.
What did you lose when you
arrived & then when you left?
She may ask this & I suggest
you tell her the truth.

◆

K. M. LIGHTHOUSE

Expanded by Sri Yantra

The mother of magic is gentle
but does not hide. The mother of magic
does not shirk when the world calls her
a stranger, when her adventure is too far removed
from this traditionalist landscape. The mother will do anything
to protect her magic, will breathe fire into words
she hands her offspring. The mother of magic walks
two millimeters above earth to remember she can,
feels all space between atoms as home
and carries this domestic love in the garden of her body.
The mother of magic will not bow when the father is wrong,
will not stop fostering what is holy as it emerges, vines up her legs,
and travels onward into the snaking folds of reality. She is the rebel
of this freedom, this witchcraft, this levity,
strange even to those who know magic,
for what she brings forth always breaks new ground
at the edge of what is and what must be. The mother of magic cures
with her poison and glides over these puddles of despondency,
moving them to the cliffside of consciousness before she dives off
in the perfect body knowledge that water will protect her
and splash only as much as shakes the ground.

♦

DAWN THOMPSON

How Does a Mother Find Time to Write a Poem?

The mother in the kitchen cutting carrots
the music of the knife on the wooden board
    click, click, click
rhyming with the first words of a poem
forming in her head

until the sound of her young son's voice
    calling

the poem flying like a small, brown bird
through the open window
        up
to the highest branch of the pear tree
where it sits for five days

until early one morning
while the mother is folding laundry
the soft oval of her husband's blue socks
remind her of the poem

the mother shuts her eyes
listens for the poem's heart beat
    tra-la, tra-la, tra-la

until the sharp cry of the doorbell
sends the poem scurrying under the living room sofa
where it hides for two weeks

Then one evening at the computer paying the bills
the mother's fingers suddenly begin typing
as if they are possessed
    by Spirits

the mother does not stop when the phone rings
the mother does not stop when the cat meows outside the closed door
the mother does not stop to check on her sleeping child

instead the wings of the mother's fingers flying
the notes of a song that will not be silenced
coming, finally, home

♦

K. M. LIGHTHOUSE

"We Must Lower Our Standard of Living So We Can Raise Our Standard of Loving"
— Ernestine Gale Konecny

And one day I find myself again
at the house of my great aunt, and here
the basement sink leaks with a dresser

against the basement door as if to keep the water out, and here
the impact mark of my father's fall
from the third stair from the top still lay decorated

with his blood and broken bits of soupbowl.
And the homeowner's insurance has not yet responded
to this accident my father is still healing from

and he knows no cleaning for himself,
so before I read him the long story of our past and future,
it falls to me to clean this house, this hearth once home to summer

poker tables and loud boasts over beer
now quiet in the healing from stroke and the silence
of the not-yet-dead. And it is here

that I pick up one ragged cloth and another and find a pushbroom
for the floor. Here, I pull a lamp forward and light candles
in the tealight holder I rescue

from behind the stove. It sits now atop the piano I dust off
where I am careful not to send cat hair and food to the swept floor.
From the top of this piano, I move my great uncle's ashes,

heavy as a body must be, and place them into the far cabinet
that houses my great-grandmother's flowered dishes. And, too,
I discover relics of flowers from distant places

40 years earlier and two crystals dug by my second cousin's hand
from tree roots and ground. And these
I set upon the long, elderly table after its clearing

and light candles there as well. As I do these things, my great aunt
speaks in her labored way, *and thank you* and *you do not know
what this means to me*, but I am content to keep cleaning

until the spices are arranged separately from supplements
and the fridge is clear of mold. And so, as if to reward this behavior,
she says, *and your great-grandmother wrote poems*

*such as you do and indeed had images flood her mind even into her age
when great events would occur,
even as when Jackie Kennedy died. And so I, too, had the images come*

when your father was first arrested.
And it is then that I recognize this great inheritance I have, and it is then
I know I must take these, my great-grandmother's poems,

and make them into something greater
even than these generations apart we are, and I must remember
who she was who lay in a coffin that carries

my first understandings of death so that our family,
here in this sleepy town such as ones where all power originates,
may remember and be remembered by all who read our words.

◆

JENN LALIME

One Day My Kitchen Will Be Clean

Counters and floors
the crumbs alone—relentless
A mountain of dishes
demand conquest each day

I sweep and swipe and scrub
but clean evades me despite
my efforts so steady
Sisyphean—you'd think

this is how she prays
clean is whom she prays to

As I work I often conjure
an old woman sipping
whiskey through a straw
standing in my clean kitchen
straining to see the tall pines
outside the window

No dishes in the sink
no eaters, no messes
Silence and solitude
the only mouths to feed
as the still broom
stands witness

Today, above this morning's
mess, I see the pines clearly
boughs swaying in the wind

♦

K. M. LIGHTHOUSE

"This Is How She Prays; Clean Is Whom She Prays To"
—Jenn Lalime

I haven't gotten out of the habit
of three showers a day, of organic produce,

of green smoothies without sugar. There is organic cotton
for wet days and oregano oil for dry ones.

I pat this body with fresh towels
cleaned with eco-friendly detergent,

and a woman I love indulges in gluten for me
while I eat sweet potatoes with pepper as complement.

The altar room is swept, the sink is empty,
and these tealights will burn for four hours,

but maybe this is not
the only type of clean my body needs.

A priestess says the spirit of her uterus
owns a broom and uses it too often, so perhaps,

while nothing that circulates is dirty,
what circulates too often does not grow.

♦

GABRIELLE HANCHER

Coming Home

I found home in the space between my legs
And it frightened me
I wasn't ready to feel again
So I disappeared into the moment between thoughts

There are days when it's too clean
So I add some dishes to the sink
Knock over a potted plant
And at least every piece of trash has it's place in the order of things

When I first met your mouth
I was caught off guard
Because it wouldn't let me leave my body,
Demanded I stay here with you, demanded I arrive fully

And now I'm washing each dish clean
Trying to capture that feeling with
My hands, my wrists, my elbows
Shoulder deep in suds, laughing amidst all these bubbles

How does it feel to be home you ask me

I am reminded of what it's like to have a soft belly
Or of the way you feel between my legs
With my heart cracked wide open
Saying *thank you thank you thank you*
Knowing that this vulnerability is just a translation
Of our hearts native tongue in symbiotic communion

And baby I'm so glad to finally be coming home again

♦

release

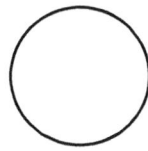

full moon

Urban Prayer

A bead of sweat
Dripping down her slender contours
Pooling in the valleys and riding angular crests
Blood on bone on wave — a journey
Until it meets the gentle flesh of the belly
Which fires the arrow ever downward

Folding forward in urban prayer
To release old stories into the mist
Which tug at the corners of her mouth
Softening the burden of containing everything
Until exhaustion spills onto the tile floor
Allowing for beauty — I am in awe

We don't meet eyes much in this space
And yet it is a space for meeting
Where we take earthly communion
With one another, slipping out of old skins
Nourishing tenderness and deep wounds
As if we could never really forget how

As if we could ever really remember
How we forgot in the first place
Or how my body turns water into wine
And yours makes meaning out of daily rituals
And this intersection of difference
Is actually where Spirit is patiently waiting

♦

Seasons

i.   **Persephone ~ Spring**

She stretches green limb
her body sprouting tulip, daffodil, crocus, iris
iris blue velvet like water
her hair, grass growing
her legs, the bodies of trees
about to bear first finger fruit
her perfume, the inside of the world
before birth, salty and sweet.

She sweeps in
her sun gown trailing insects
awakened by thaw
ready to till love into clod of dirt so
beauty can rise from mud
color can open from thin air
life can return after even the harshest of freeze.

ii.   Moon Medicine ~ Summer

She lowers the pail into the well
pulls up black water
a full bucket of it
sets it on the grass to moon bathe until dawn

She has heard tell water painted by the moon
gives you the power to change
loosens old skin and masks
tightened by days of trying

She has heard tell water soaked in the moon's gaze
becomes the sweet nectar
of free life
free thought
liberation

Under the fits and starts of summer stars she waits
and when morning finally comes
eagerly tips the metal lip to her mouth
lets the moon dusted river
rush her body
clear her of all things caged

iii.　　The Turning ~ Autumn

Autumn weighs her losses
in scarlet, burnt pumpkin, fading yellow.
She stands vigil
on the threshold of season,
her long red hair
a fire through the forest
burning the old fruit of the year
to ash
so that when you breathe
death is in your mouth.

Even the squirrel knows it is time
to hibernate the nuts,
which fall like so many moons.

iv.   Sleep ~ Winter

The great iceberg of her body.
The mountain peak of her longing.
The deep, cold drifts of her loss.
The winter storm of her love.
hush child
hush
Snow is falling.

♦

What Now?

1.

It's November, 2016
and even though my father had voted for a man he wouldn't leave
his granddaughter alone in room with
(or at least shouldn't leave his granddaughter alone in a room with)
>*you left me in plenty of rooms with plenty such men*

and my brother voted this way
and almost half of my country voted this way
I still believed that the sharp pain in my core was overblown
a bit neurotic because I've always felt a little bit alone in this
overblown and neurotic: *the* feminist among the feminists
>*this isn't right, this is everywhere*

asking my strongest women
>*how can you breathe?*

getting shoulder shrugs and
"What do you do?"
"What about the poor men?"
"Women give just as good as they get"
and I wanted to believe them, believe it wasn't that bad
that I was overreacting—
>*who am I to accuse, indict an entire gender?*

I had no idea how safe this

                                          allaloneness

made me feel because I've a mind for science, for facts
for probability, so if it's only me who felt held down
(even when nobody was physically holding me down)
and it's only me who squirmed, reading hunger in all those eyes
that should have been on the presentation
the project plan, the spreadsheet
only me who saw the dismissive looks of male friends
(and the downcast eyes of their wives)

                                          don't rock the boat

after a few drinks and speaking of one thing
just one of the million things that had happened
or the anger in my brother's eyes
when I stated simple facts about the ways I've been compromised
his wife's been compromised, his niece is compromised

Maybe it was just me who knew how to kill a conversation
with any man by mere mention of sexism,
harassment, telling of any part of my story
the shyest assertion of my reality—

let alone the well of fear and anger

never show the anger

only me who sat sad and stunned at how quickly

even the good guys change the subject

If its only me or a just a handful who believes in this boogey man

then I could also believe, in my more rational moments

that he doesn't exist at all

2.

It's October, 2017
and women are speaking and their words wash away
the blanket of rationalizations, so many women—

me too and me too and me too

story after story, all beautifully told and horrifyingly nuanced
the ways the delicate strings of these women's power

even the powerful women

were plucked and pulled and cut
and all I can think was I was right

I didn't want to be right

I prefer thinking and feeling I was a bit crazy

oversensitive

but now here it is—your worst belly fear all over the front page

your fear is the world
your daughter's world

I did not want to be right
(as much as I had thought I wanted to be)
wanted confirmation that I indeed had to be
so much more to be offered so much less

I realized I did not want my truth

to be the truth

because what now?

3.
It's September, 2018
and I'm learning how to breathe all over again
in my truth

that is the truth

and to love and trust my father and my brother
and my husband anew

even if they still don't speak fluent truth

And the nation in free fall with the man—

the living breathing boogey man

still pulling the strings

Change for him and his comes too fast

oh, the good old days

appointing his kind, his mirror
hanging him in the highest court

that will now hang us

blame us, strip us for a generation

For those of us who held the truth

before the truth held us

change comes at a glacial pace
and while there are victories, days that feel like *yes*

there are more days that feel like all we are doing
is handing the wolves sheep's clothes
drawing lines we hope they do not cross
but when the power is still in pants
and those pioneers poised to change it all
                                    still aren't the right woman
still aren't believed
the moment feels precarious
whispers about darker days ahead
how safe can it really be on the other side of an invisible fence?

♦

Addendum to Blood Moon Eclipse Over The Pacific

After Peter Hujar/Candy Darling

She's going to drop half
unmasked, before she's fully revealed,
one hand holding faithfully, the red fruit
of the worlds' shadow, while still
clutching white sheets & gripping
the back of the chair used for formal
portraits—blood painting her eyelids,
the black, the white aesthetic relentless.

If you change postures she changes appearance.
From down on the sidewalk or in middle
street the earth seems so very ripe. Yet
from the weight of the mascara night—
there remains one single rose on the felt
pilled flannel blanket, the sole
punctuation needed for elegy . . . and you know
we weep, we all do while way up in each
airplane someone is wondering about us,
way down here on the ground.

What from the city can be truly seen
of the night sky—its rambunctious
nothingness, the frame holding stars
phantom light shearing each of our faces?
It does no good to kill anyone, or to pose.
Man or woman—man with his
lifelines, woman with her hinge
to the underworld—the mouth to the sea.
She will fall into it anyhow, we will—
half disguised, half discovered, flaunting
our little shocks of brilliance against
the wet lips of death—what it is to shine
just so, to love this contrast, tethered
& smoky with vain expressions,
but somehow free, freely listening
to the big rock opera, that strange
pure roaring amplification
of our hungers.

◆

BETH MELNICK

Stars Fall Down

There was a time before leaf slush
stuck to his boots.
Before rain drenched his sleeping bag—
the bag he now wears on his endless, sleepless walk

through streets and more rain.
Sodden streets,
the sleeping bag his royal cape.
He greets subjects invisible to us.

Were we to walk in that melting newspaper cap
and heavy cape
would its magical properties
bestow themselves upon us?

The boots come from different mothers,
not even twins.
The hair reaches up—
a crown to meet grey sky.
The king of our street has returned.

He mumbles the royal language
and barks at anyone who addresses him directly.

He lives on air
and incantations.
He takes nothing offered him.
He turns this way and that, followed by the heavy folds.

The hands cross his body, providing the clasp.
The eyes dart and fall upon his subjects.
He stands motionless now,
on that corner, just there,
waiting to be transported.

Stars fall down
and become transports for small boys
sleeping in the woods.

They fight battles,
darting in and out of trees,
speeding home for dinner
in warm kitchens.

A mother's rough hand pushes
tendrils of hair from a round flushed cheek.
A boy encircled by soft arms
is laid in a warm bed
and awakens the king of a busy street corner.

♦

Solstice

It is the shortest day of the year and the longest night. Shadows have long since vacated the premises but there is comfort in the blackness. I lean in, peering into the darkness, looking for an edge with which to cast, but there is only a single beckoning flame which draws me nearer. I am wearing the darkness bravely, like a blanket, my feet lighter than a moth's wing as I am drawn inward. I can hear her singing, blowing dust from her lungs, hands drumming purposefully against thighs. The sweetness of it soothes me and suddenly we are together on the hearth. Her shoulders sag a little but her eyes are unmistakable twin flames dancing merrily. She is touching my hands and I am leaning in to listen, caught between the softness of dark's embrace and the warmth of her whispers. She tells me everything knowing I will forget. There is sweetness and I am reminded of eating sticky raspberries in the summertime. I am dreaming. She tucks hair behind my ears, letting one wrinkled hand cup my cheeks tenderly. *There will be sadness too, my love. But remember that the light always returns.*

♦

JENN LALIME

For Hye

I can't tell you
what will hurt you—
what will taste most ripe

But I can shore you
as you discover both—
as you writhe and savor

I can't tell you
how two people
so complicate love

But I can listen
as you examine how
you did, how you heal

I can't tell you
where the mines lay—
paving each road as they do

But I can help
map the terrain—
survey the days ahead

I can't tell you
everything will be okay
it won't be, until it is

But I can wait
long days and nights
until the quickening

I can't tell you
where to go—where you will go
nor can I follow

But I can stand
sentinel—my arms
wide open and waiting

♦

HOLADAY MASON

The Dying are Good Children to the Dead

Your ribs crackle, each breath fevered as a living wren buried under snow.

You are the only woman you will become & now you are undone in even that,

preferring morphine tonight to peppermint, which scalds your tongue & calls up thoughts of old lovers.

Still, what a diamond moon this last night, the color of departure as it circles in the heights.

And the lights of distant houses floating like parachutes against the obsidian mountain.

Your gift to me is your burning skin. Mine to you—two freezing hands imprinting the dried documents of your cheeks with my lifeline. Yes,

I will go on awhile longer, I suspect.

As a girl I made a habit of running at night through the crookedness of unfamiliar landscapes testing the wingspan of my terror.

& on tough bare-feet I ran over fire *just once*, before the dismemberments of time—the scarred twin lodge poles of my legs, bones hoary lace now titanium pruned by the whittling of the years.

Our silver hairs fall & fly like rustling ceremonial flags. I bow to you.

We were here once!

I will bank the silence of your sealed mouth like embers so you can travel without worry. The things of life go on.

This is your one & only moment to be consumed by the profound solitude of dying.

In the room beyond your bed, the mid-winter table is decorated with
unseasonable magnolias—blooms born of mud & jeweled beetles,
the flowers arranged, huge

as children's faces, around your favorite hand-painted plate,
the one with English roses falling towards the center, away from
the edges.

♦

gratitude

waning gibbous moon

GABRIELLE HANCHER

A New Look

It is the sigh escaping your lips, and I am through this domestic gateway. All of these worries are the heavy coats I didn't intend to wear so I am checking mine at the door and arriving. When I look over my shoulder, the blind spots are starting to radiate finally and what I reflect back to you is a kind of honesty reserved only for ink or consensual bruises. I am peeling away the things that are too tight, the things that are familial hand-me-downs and I trade them in for something I've clumsily knitted myself. And you are too. I can see you trying to decide if all the holes in your shirt mean it's time for something new, even though you might feel comfortable in the cold. So I offer you my compassionate silence, cover you in it like a warm blanket in the hopes that I can meet you exactly where you're at. And we lean in, admiring our mismatched socks and bold attire like god damn royalty. I hold you while you hold your shirt, making space so when the deep rift happens you're allowed to fall with the knowing my arms will catch you. That I am still falling, too, but that we are whole even so. I want my wardrobe to scream free, and you're learning that, too. As this moment arises, you've never looked more beautiful to me, more comfortable in the clothes of your choosing. That other shit doesn't fit anymore and we fall laughing into our pile of costumes and clothes.

♦

ASH GOOD

When Women Circle‡

> *"Believe me, in the future someone will remember us..."*
> —Sappho

We toss lines into the open
like flowers‡, she muses.
I broke the pattern‡
and other words we whisper.
There is no fire in this circle
only in our centers—some that
grow babies and some that
never will and some that
may still—all mothers. We whisper
mothering one another,
our own words back. *Like flowers*
the priestess muses—piled in the center.

‡ *In gratitude to the words of Kristen Roderick, Dawn Thompson & Jewelie Randall*

◆

RHONDA NICHOLS

Winter Circle

I would like to remember
How it felt in our first gathering
The newness of your faces
The sound of your words
The reverence of silence and one breath

I would like to remember
The words offered that landed
At the feet of my soul
And answered questions
I wasn't ready to ask

As I reflect on winter
Reaching for more light
Our darkest day is passing
I feel welcomed and ready
For the words that desire life

♦

DAWN THOMPSON

The Crone Gives a Pedicure

She motions me to place my feet
in the waters.
I can see she is the boss.

She is the woman of years
amongst the young roses
who paint the toenails of women
    who wish
for just an hour
to be treated like a Queen.

The Crone speaks another language.
The sisters of her hands lift my feet,
    one by one,
as if they are her children.

The power in her hands
    is old.
It is the trunk of an oak tree,
the wisdom of moonlight.

She knows I do not treat myself to these things often.
She rubs the bottom of my feet where the lumps are,
where all the sorrow and pain live.

I let what she offers in and
    toe by toe,
she plucks the old out and away.

She is not stingy with her time.
She understands the need to
sometimes
be loved by a stranger, to
sometimes
say yes to simple pleasures.

◆

I Don't Know You

but I know your wisdom, dear woman. That undulating that rises from womb space, that chamber of access, that well spring of potential. That memory of moving body, clarity of energy. How you hoist what is yours out of the ground. How you move in defiant joy to the error that suggests it is not your birthright. We might call this dance but I fear too few would expand that movement to include the winged energy-being you discover, gently cup in your hands. To include the reclamation process, the unearthing of how holy lives in body. I can barely know myself but I know our wisdom dear women. How these shifting monoliths taproot intuition. I choose to bow to your source before I judge those jaunting branches, how leaves fall around you. So that under soil, under skin, under our music is where quiet power is. I understand, dear woman, how vulnerable it is to reveal your naked warrior. The eye contact required after.

♦

Ancient Mother

Beckoned
By the scent of her bouquet
Wild roses pink and tender

She's in a hurry today
Rushing with others
Toward a big celebration
I'm not a part of

I ponder her beginning
One snowflake in winter
High above the dwellings
Where man busies himself
With the toils that come to nothing

I wish I could join her
Over smooth boulders
And deep pools
Where jeweled scales
Wait for a winged body's pause
Then strike with a flash of sunlight
Falling back into darkness

I hear her sing of freedom
And the urgency of living
Until time has passed
The baton of wonder
To the next in line like royalty

Those privileged with hours
To rest against her grassy breast
Watch her green crown sparkle
As she dashes on

◆

LAUREN PAREDES

Suddenly Every Sound is a Love Song

Between At Last and sigh
the abrupt flight of a December raven
a heart hearing affirmations for the first time
         and believing
     It's in the comfort of a rhyme scheme
    a stranger's suggestion to make the moon
      the mother you greet each evening

what you will say in two weeks' time
upon cracking open a door
to find that your wings have arrived
        the sound of unwrapping

♦

forgiveness

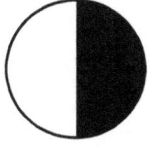

last quarter moon

ASH GOOD

Her Cosmos of Hearths, This Settling

she remembers
her place when she is given the first taste &

other matters she discovers
cannot be trusted to imperfect humans

so for a time she mistakes
she must go alone

unaccustomed to quiet
sure she glimpses a companion at the counter

who isn't there but is perhaps
spirit

she has forgotten
she is not alone

in this cavern of her sounds
forehead furrowed & cheekbones in blue light

she remembers
her place sitting equal among men

how she invokes the mother
though she is not one in this body & these men never will be

her relief when at least one elder recounts
the tale of the crone who watches over

his small child body running in flower beds
in summer on the same land her child self does

home is the comfort of a stranger who knows
the invisible history of the groundwater she drinks

she remembers
her place in long grass

how she cannot speak to the sentries of this land
because no one can teach her those names

she remembers
her place

during the longest night
the ancients sit beside her while the sky fires light

♦

HOLADAY MASON

Winter Solstice: The Last View

In the house of the body—
a window, a door.
I disappear through each.
And the roof is always red.

I remember the blood years,
the clotted indigo, the inside,
then out, determined seeds,
seasons like fleet antelope—

Once a red headed Indian man
stole me from the fecund valley,
drove me hard to North Fork
where he made up for his harm
with a new doeskin, a rattler's hide.

Once a man lied that he was
unable to fuck, then laid claim
to my generosity anyhow. Once,
I threw my body off a rock wall
to turn a guitar into a man
who would love me.

I've broken all the gemstones between
my back molars to turn a man red
in the bath, watching him
sadly wilt in the water, running as
a woman in my tight headscarf
& precious battery operated lamp
seeking the way by sheer will.

In the house of the body
the years past & the mirrors
of time keep showing me the country
where friends die then regard
themselves reflecting
in my memories as they muse —
how funny we are,
all of us hiding in the thickets.

In the house of the boy is a man.
In the house of the woman: a girl.
In the windows are the forever pale
vistas immediate with dissolution,
like separating twins—
my knees are so cold.

A younger me was caught waving
to myself here in this window
studying the face I would become,
while my brother, still alive,
played his steel guitar to charm women—
to call our father home—we two,
still tender as new rabbits.

Then, I was like you now,
a hollow of gold honey nether
hair & blood, wanting babies,
with every moon, climbing
the moon. Imagine what
I saw up there.

In each room of the house
of the body curls a specific
animal remembering its nature
by attending its own smell.

In the rooms of my body
I open the doors.
I open the windows.
I climb a ladder to the roof.
I have no choice.
As it is, everything is magic.

♦

GABRIELLE HANCHER

On the Subject of Self Care

The space between each breath is weighted heavy
    i am small
the memory claws its way into the present
and then the spiraling begins
we are free falling
and this void feels loud and familiar
As i descend i hear Her and this time, this time
dissociation dissolves into somatic kaleidoscope

So i'm a student down here, all wide eyed in the darkness
    But i don't know how to love this way yet
i stare down at the bassinet, at the screaming babe
to notice the trembling slope in Her shoulders
curled to protect a heart so precious it can hardly stand to beat
the fury in Her sweaty wrinkled brow
the way Her jaw is a busted cage,
grinding away at loneliness already
but this time i'm here, and the lifeline keeps me tethered
So i reach down carefully and smooth back Her damp hair
massage Her tiny shaking fists,
holding on so tightly to the blanketed darkness
where someone was supposed to be

I pick Her up (even though it doesn't come naturally)
    Not all mothers are born knowing how to love
And We lean in together,
holding on tightly,
letting go loosely
until We're humming the same lullaby
and dreaming the same soothing dream
both remembering what it's like
to cradle Wisdom in the dark

♦

JENN LALIME

What Follows

My father speaks of poems
written to his first-true-love—
not my mother

never my mother.
His words, countless letters
sealed and sent from Hampton

Harbor to Puget Sound.
Exhilarating, this love—
older than I and true.

His blue eyes betray pain.
I shift, remember how deep
down love can burrow in a man.

He'd followed her words
across a continent
traded sunrise for sunset

only to find his beloved
taken up with another.
This would be love's lesson—

meeting my mother
the spark, crushed again
living love in the flesh

each long day.
But then you were born
he smiles, glances sideways at me.

Heartbreak remains
in the small space between us—
we leave it there to burn.

◆

Mercury Moves Like a Stone Rolled in Front of the Cave

The repeat of hair needing brushed, put up off the neck, dry shampooed, brushed again, how I enjoy these tangles but not yesterday's. Clean hair starts a new cycle with no texture.

How he wakes me. How I wake him. How this sleepy moment in defiance of an alarm is freedom's quintessence.

The ticking time bomb of perfect length nails, how going one hour too long will leave the longest torn down to a pink bed.

The resistance in solving the dripping sink for good. The repeated effort to pour out the pan collecting the water.

The inconsequential realnesses of body. The constant evaluation of thinness, too loose neck skin, a spot that may or may not be malignant. What am I pretending is real?

Gran is getting older, hearing phantom scanner calls and getting surprised by news another friend has died. I will forgive this confetti of emotion. When I am not broken, what does healing look like?

♦

Worthy

What if my words were worthy
to bear the weight of silence
reflected in the eyes of suffering?

What if my words cupped and gentle
held cool water to parched lips?
Would they be worthy then?

What if words illuminated the doubt
of heartbeats in isolation,
trapped by circumstances
chosen in compassion
before enduring became the only thing?

What if I ignore the gift within,
when one voice is all it takes
to touch the hollow longing
we shoulder into darkness?

Words can listen
Hands together
In shared humanity

♦

ASH GOOD

"My Mother's Voice, That Imperfect Love"
—Holaday Mason

she is raised on the mother's shoulders
& now when she wants the mother to remain

unaged & strong
the mother's body instead softens

sculpted in part by her weight
this cannot be undone

in the sigh that follows she catches herself
exhaling the sound of the mother

this cannot be undone
only she is newly free each visit

♦

surrender

waning crescent moon

RHONDA NICHOLS

Annie

My hand lightly caressing
Your soft snowy coat
Your body now a bony shadow
Heaving
Ragged breath of goodbye

You wait
I wait
For the heartbeat to still
With eyes no longer seeing

Seven years of antics
Burrowing under blankets
Finding the hidden treats
Of our unsuspecting guest

We chose this journey
Adopted in winter
You were my comfort
In the storms of teenage angst

Your excited twirling
Puppy like bounce
Slowed with the dying
But I won't forget

Farewell my beloved
Your spirit now set free
Let me feel you in the silence
Prancing through the trees

♦

DAWN THOMPSON

The Beloved

For months afterwards
you look for the Beloved everywhere

You think you see him
in the green-breasted hummingbird at the feeder
outside the kitchen window

There he is in a swirl of Autumn leaves
rising like a phoenix at a Stop sign

When you touch his hand of stone
you know immediately
whatever made him your father
has flown

this body him
but not him
this body a noble boat
tossed   and tossed   and tossed
by the greatest of storms

now
so still
now
so full of echoes

Your father dies one day before
your 52nd birthday
and that is a gift somehow

It's all a gift you decide
the long years of cancer
the last gray months of going

all the miracles
all the moments of
Love   Love   Love in between

You plant a burning bush
outside your bedroom window
for the Beloved

You speak with the Beloved at night
as you fall asleep

You think about all the years that
prepared you for this
but when it finally comes
it is much too soon

the father
        the Beloved
the father
        the Beloved

the body
the burning bush
the unbearable gift

♦

BETH MELNICK

The Circle

I will do your crying for you.

I will hold you in my heart and let the river flow.

We will cast a net to hold it, all of it, and we will hold you.
We will hold you and the love will pour though us,
our hair, our skin, our every cell.

We will catch the pain with our net and transmute it
with our love.

We will hold this circle as long as necessary,
'til every tear is shed ...

And the clouds thin and part, and, as after a great thunder storm,
the light cracks the grey ... and long after.

We will hold you in the gentle fabric of our circle.

When we part it is not a coming apart.
It is a widening, an expansive opening to the air,
the sun, to birds, fish, all manner of animals and plants.
We can hold all this with our love.
We can hold you and all that you bring.

There is not a part of you that cannot be held here,
in this circle, in this space, at this moment
and forever.

♦

Something Heroic About Curling Into a Fetal Position to Hold the Multiverse Under the Bed

for Beth

she trades all she knows to breathe
open an intercostal portal

undone rippling
out of walls

until doors-down neighbors
are vaguely suspicious

legs parted at the threshold
in and out of body

heavy on another room's floor
unsure of when or how she time travels

to watch herself
now in the pose of child

waterbearer to the ocean that is hers   the mother's
the woman-at-the-market's she will never speak to

her vital hum in deference
over-swollen for this container

of fingernails
armpit hair & saliva

♦

JENN LALIME

Right in Front of You

It was the broken parts
you came to love
that bound you

cracked your heart
open—invited you
to touch, to inhabit

That first intimate pair
leafless, without shame—
do you remember?

And now on the interstate
late getting home
not calling to say:

I'm sorry, I'm coming, I'm
dripping with love for you—
I'll never leave like that again

Was it a snake? A stranger
a familiar, digital creep
whispering doubt—tempting?

Or did you weaponize
what you saw there
in the wide open heart of her

sink your teeth into apple—
glistening and sweet and
right in front of you?

Surely you remember Eden,
but are you brave enough
to bare yourself anew?

Inevitable perhaps
    —inhala, exhala—

that we leave love there
on the floor between us
like a cup that rolled under the couch.

♦

LAUREN PAREDES

Be Soft a Little Longer

Lesson One: What would you do
if someone said they were
'dripping with love' for you?

*I wouldn't mind escaping to the ocean
and not telling anyone. Accepting love
seems like such a task this evening.*

Answer: Too much water.
I prefer armadillo shells & tumbleweeds.
Environs inhospitable to curious fingertips.

*Once I dreamt of guerilla open-heart surgery.
I had to trick my captor into putting
my organ back where it belongs.*

Lesson Two: Explore
your damp emptiness.
Report on its contents.

> *I've been schooled to behold a truth:*
> *we must crack our chests open—*
> *disfigure what's inside—to know with precision.*

Answer: The sweet honeysuckle
of surrender, fear turning now
a warm amber.

◆

K. M. LIGHTHOUSE

In These Nested Eggs, May We Never Harden

Monthly cramps are worse now,
now that I am older and healthy and wake up
at five a.m. to bursting pain

from a left ovary, terrified this isn't normal.
I wake a lover with squirms, ask
for ibuprofen from the car as if I am pregnant

insisting on middle-of-the-night Cheetos,
and since I am infertile,
this is my favor.

The pain doesn't leave, so my lover asks
what color it is,
how much water can it hold,

what animal is it, and suddenly I know
there is story inside this egg—imagine it as a baby penguin
cold on its mother's feet, afraid as it taps with a beak

that may never break shell open. My lover asks, *what emotion
is it; what does it want?* I croak *love, warmth,
encouragement* and return

to sleep while my lover holds this egg and ovary
in a cupped hand ahead of a brimming dawn.
Wake again, and the pain's gone,

but I offer cups and cups of blood to water
on the solstice when it is all right
that this eggshell has not brittled, that this beak

is not fully formed, that the open world
will wait
so I can stay this soft

a while longer.

♦

Menopause

The pause of the blood, the not now
or ever impasse of womb, iron of emptiness,
the buried plasma roots of beginning,
the end of the eggs, the un-union of skin,
the played out tryst, the staunched
memory, stolen heirloom, scarred
slit wrist, the un-hatched, un-cried,
dried blown out wisp of smoke, the sealed eye,
silenced tome, floating black fish,
un-made unmade bed, the cessation
of red, the blank rivulet, the witch's song
inside the deaf nest—ten young
drowning men in the surf. One on his belly,
a newborn clinging to his back, screaming.

♦

BETH MELNICK

They Stepped Back Into the Arms of the Infinite

They stepped back
into the arms of the infinite—
gracious arms and hands
that strip away all filters.

From the safety of that embrace
they watched the film of their
life on earth.

They laughed and cried and when offered
the possibility of return.
They politely declined.

♦

beginning

●

new moon

Rebirth

The days grow longer
Like a yawn
Stretching arms and legs
As the sky holds her tears
And I walk
Ears still covered for warmth

Sweet smell of Daphne
Pink with promise
Change is coming
Bare earth stirring as green bodies
Boldly show some skin

Dried old bulbs
Lose their slumber
Become young again
With the return of sun

I await their colorful heads
Lining my driveway
I buried them on my knees

A child with a spade
To remember
As her memory fades

She taught me to love yellow
And the coming of spring
How to be a mother
To stretch my wings

♦

LAUREN PAREDES

"It's All a Gift, You Decide"
—Dawn Thompson

The fluctuating light
      the purple darkness
before the metamorphosis

      the wildflower path just beyond
your sight
        Even the raven pivoting to lamppost

      the moth lost before a midnight burial
the phantom cat who nuzzled your fist instead
      are all trying to tell you something of miracles

      This gift is the last essence of resistance
you had in your being
      before new doubt hatchlings surely

Surely this was all always meant for you

♦

ASH GOOD

Until the Notion of Other Cannot Be Parsed Separate at All

after Ellen Bass

this has all happened before
she finds herself a bewildered thing in a middle-aged woman's body

stirring for how the mother must have once looked at her
this is a poem she knows

a poem that has more than once prayed she question
echoes in a single brain sliver

one over the other like vellum
how many sunrises she suckles

until she makes the first memory
this has all happened before

she finds herself a nascent thing in a crone's body certain
this is a poem she knows

a poem that has more than once prayed she question
one quantum jump from dependency

of childhood to the impatience of long distance love
her share of airport kisses

the first ways she is licked by touch
so her lips mother

a poem she knows—
louisiana motel room instead of senior prom

she is not a meditator yet but lays like she is nothing
but a heart

beat in veins reduced to the lazy spin of fan blades
humid southern air throbs louder

than the scratch of an extended stay blanket
still until you ask if she is there & even then

still
she unearths her pulse for the first time

mistakenly credits origin to outside stimulus
this has all happened before

once more
this poem she knows

she finds herself an ancient thing in a young girl's body freely
sourcing this power

♦

GABRIELLE HANCHER

The Alchemist

She told me there is light running through my body—through the spine. And I am practicing this strange alchemy—hearing the way light transforms to darkness and back to light. Fingers to nose and I watch the serpents coil tighter towards each other, feel their soft curling scales create scaffolding around vitality. When I open my mouth, rivers and tributaries pour out, but this time I'm not shoveling the water back in. Something vibrates back to me, and suddenly I can harmonize truthfully. I realize the snakes are actually unborn sentences, racing to meet the epicenter of all that is good in me. And then our hands are meeting in holy palmers' kiss—I cannot contain what joy feels like in my own skin so I'm giving it to you. I am so full of unborn sentences. You receive my creation as if you have always known what being alive sounds like—as if witnessing light becoming matter is simply a thing one does.

♦

HOLADAY MASON

When She

When she says he told her what she offered
was perfectly what he needed, when hearing this

was what she needed, when the circle of baldly
tender words set adrift a field of blinking pastel

lanterns, when the matching allegory stones
found their way to the pair bonded lovers

wrists, when she whispered *my beloved is forever,
forever is my beloved*, before she said, *I am happy*

*in this little house, wearing the old turquoise
necklace, my belly now just like my mother's—*

when the avocado tree clicked with dust &
blue mourning doves chortled, when she surveyed

her immaculate kitchen before the task
of chopping onions, when the freezing muddy

creek rose with no damage to the cottonwoods,
when all the rose & green umbrellas tilted

so rain didn't put out the candles, when she
lay her head down on the table to test the weight

of dying, when she rose & walked to the corner
candy store for a simple piece of ginger, when the end

of the year arrived & she vowed she would be silent,
when she broke the promise while applying Moca

lipstick, when everyone was fed & no one grumbled,
when all friends agreed they'd forgive the year its crimes,

when she said she valued crows as well as ravens,
the ones that carried the seasons to their horizon,

when she watched closely over whatever she could
attend, when the winter bed was heaped with blankets,

when vision cleared & she could see perfections
rippling tidepools, when she noted no one had been

forgotten, when she said what he offered was perfect,
he was perfectly what she needed. When they finally slept.

♦

biographies

ASH GOOD was born in Paradise, California, and raised in a small Oregon mill town. She is the author of *we are not ready for what we are, sounds in my möbius mind* (First Matter Press) and *These things will never happen quite like that again* (LettersAt3AMPress). Ash is a book designer, the initiatrix of High Priestesses of Poetry and a facilitator for Portland Women Writers where she holds sacred space for story tellers to connect with their inner healer and highest self. She lives in Portland, Oregon. *ashgood.com*

BETH MELNICK is committed to the practice of writing a short thing almost every day. She is a Reiki Master and photographer who has enjoyed a long, accidental, career spanning over 25 years as a location scout and manager for film and still photography. This work has opened doors to other realities and intimately engaged her with people and situations she would never otherwise have known. Sometimes she writes about them. Beth lives with her husband and son in Portland, Oregon.

DAWN THOMPSON oversees and facilitates writing workshops and retreats through Portland Women Writers, a writing collective fostering creativity, transformation, healing and connection. She also holds a weekly writing circle through the Knight Cancer Institute at OHSU for women healing from cancer.

Dawn believes writing our stories is a sacred act that liberates, heals and transforms us. She is passionate about how writing in community offers us the gift of becoming more intimate with our self and more connected to one another. When not in a writing circle Dawn spends precious time with her husband, son and circle of family, most often in the great outdoors, and is a passionate participant of Master's Track & Field. *pdxwomenwriters.com*

GABRIELLE HANCHER is a high priestess, creator, and expressive mover from the Portland area. As a writer, she is passionate about mindfully exploring the intersection between trauma and hope. When she isn't crafting word magic, practicing yoga, or pole dancing around town, you can find her curled up at home in pajamas watching cartoons and reading queer YA graphic novels with her husband Steven and cat Luna.

HOLADAY MASON is author of *The Red Bowl*, *Dissolve*, *Towards the Forest* and *The Weaver's Body;* co-author of *The "She" Series: A Venice Correspondence*; and three times a Pushcart nominee. Widely published, she is also a fine art photographer living in Venice with the flocks of wild green parrots. *holadaymasonphotography.com / holadaymason.com*

JENN LALIME is a lover of story in all its forms—as a writer, a founding editor of *Voicecatcher*, and an Integral Coach, her life's work is deepening her own voice and amplifying the voices of others. While travels with her brood have taken her to over 25 countries, she is most at home in the forests of the Pacific Northwest.

K. M. LIGHTHOUSE graduated from the University of Utah and worked as the senior poetry director of *enormous rooms* for two years but has since made the Pacific Northwest a home. The poet's other works appear in *From Sac*, *Blue Lake Review*, and *Toasted Cheese*, as well as two chapbooks entitled *You Are an Ambiguous Pronoun* and *The Observer Effect*. K. M. is an assistant organizer with Portland's Eastside Poetry Workshop and co-founder of First Matter Press. She serves as priestess for portals of intuitive knowledge in community by providing writing and workshop spaces for self-healing, offering tools for conscious body movement and tantric dance, and holding integration ceremonies. She channels her intuition in both energy work and energy play. K. M. is a polyamorous queer woman intent on living vulnerably and laying groundwork for others to live similarly in their own power. *kmlighthouse.com*

LAUREN PAREDES is a storyteller across mediums with a soft spot for the unusual. She is particularly fond of the magic that happens when women come together to share (and find) their voices. Lauren currently resides in Portland, Oregon where she is a founding member of the Eastside Poetry Workshop and First Matter Press Collective. Her debut chapbook, *Otherwise, Magic (*First Matter Press) was released in March 2019.

RHONDA NICHOLS is the mother of two grown daughters and found her poetic voice in her mid-thirties. A deep soul, she has found the emotional release of writing the best avenue to process the complexities of life. Rhonda has a Bachelor of Science degree in Housing Studies from Oregon State University and works as a personal companion to clients with profound memory loss. Her poem "Old Men" was published in *The Museletter*. Additional poems can be found in *Poems of July: A Collection*. She lives in Tigard, Oregon with her husband and mother.

www.ingramcontent.com/pod-product-compliance
Lightning Source LLC
Chambersburg PA
CBHW082216090526
44584CB00025BA/3770